Radius of Light

JOSHUA AUERBACH

Radius of Light

LIVRES DC BOOKS

Cover illustration by Olivier Lasser. Author photograph by Amelia Marley. Book designed and typeset by Primeau & Barey, Montreal. Edited by Steve Luxton.

Legal Deposit, *Bibliothèque et Archives nationales du Québec* and the National Library of Canada, 4th trimester, 2007.

Library and Archives Canada Cataloguing in Publication
Auerbach, Joshua, 1968-
Radius of light/Joshua Auerbach.
Poems.
ISBN 978-1-897190-34-0 (pbk.)
ISBN 978-1-897190-35-7 (bound).
I. Title.
PS8601.U372R34 2007 C811'.6 C2007-906659-3

For our publishing activities, DC Books gratefully acknowledges the financial support of the Canada Council for the Arts, of SODEC, and of the Government of Canada through the Book Publishing Industry Development Program (BPIDP).

Canada Council for the Arts · Conseil des Arts du Canada · Société de développement des entreprises culturelles Québec

Printed and bound in Canada by Marquis Imprimeur. Interior pages printed on 100 per cent recycled and FSC certified Silva Enviro 110 white paper. Distributed by LitDistCo.

DC Books
PO Box 666, Station Saint-Laurent
Montreal, Quebec H4L 4V9
www.dcbooks.ca

This book is dedicated to
Mikhael Dylan Auerbach.

Many people have aided
In putting together this final version: thanks
To my friends, fellow writers
Who have offered suggestions, and
To my family, above all.

Special thanks to Steve Luxton
for indefatigably bringing
this manuscript to publication,
and to my grandmother
Frances Miller for inspiration.

Contents

Over there, the river-
bank is rising against us;
a black-lit
micro-mass–

Paul Celan

Mankind is a dream of a shadow.
But when a god-given brightness comes,
a radiant light rests on men,
and a gentle life.

Pindar

Slant of Light

Jaundiced is the note that sings out in terror
When life denies the presence of light. Day shines
And light pours like a slant of God's rays. Here in
The moment, away from traffic and distractions, your
Cells metastasize. Light-giving energies sway,
Yet through it all, serenity grows. It is here, in this
Center-being, that sees the birth
Of stars, once again life will follow, once more
Salt void and teeming fullness
Find their home. To dark nebulae
And from bottomless oceans, we say *good-bye,*
And I, your provenance-dweller, your resident *in situ*
For these precious days, say "Godspeed," "Health." For
The crossing over. For the obviating of pain. For all that is.

Dance of the Arrogant Bee

Flowers open
I hover in the air
Circle

The hive is crazy for yellow

I spiral by petals
Beware of my razor point
My proboscis dips &
Pulls out primrose nectar

I sink farther into pollen, my legs covered with granules
Then on to the next iridescent blossom

Back to jelly, honeycomb, wax
& hives made of sweet nature's root

When we cluster, I dance a song
Spill into mellifluous antics
Of the summer swarm

No other buzzing above the earth gathers
Such sweet clover
Sending shivers down children's spines

Song of the Lament

(Translation of Federico Garcia Lorca's
Casida del llanto)

I have closed my balcony
Because I do not want to hear weeping,
But from behind grey stone,
Nothing is heard but weeping.

Only a few angels are singing,
Only a few dogs barking,
A thousand violins in the palm of my hand.

Because the weeping is a giant dog,
The weeping is a thousand-voiced angel,
Tears close the wind's mouth
And nothing is heard but weeping.

Ash

The wind is broken like a child's shattered glass, or
Rilke's *Malte Laurids Brigge*–shards of anxiety:
Pieces do not fit together, no whole.
An echo subsides, suddenly inert.
When we begin do we fail, or do we
Still in the night the beat of another, the rustle of twig
Or stem or bole cracked in rattled light? This life is
No easy furtherance, no sudden twist to make
Things meet. The hand that you hold
Is yours on loan, only yours for a second
To fathom the distance that separates you
From your self, from the flashes of stars called night.

Spirit Intrusion: Herniated Disc

Divinity breaks, knocks, blows and breathes
Into my body, my shattered bone:

Heft of silence filled with sounds
Of space, and whispers. The gulls and crows
Circle overhead, daily, hourly,
The black ash crows win. My rapt

Body moves with the tic
Of an insect, a wing flutter
That displaces bone, displaces column:

Vertebrae, strength. A bug
That marrows my body into lopsidedness,
The gesture of a blind man begging.

Hive

I

While I could have lit the fire
You stood motionless,
Silent, syllables locked

A soft tongue pressed to a hard-stop
Become this; transform into that.
I grab your hand, gather

Red-veined seeds for planting
Our arms lift out of clay
Pails fill with pebbles & quartz

Scores of bees seek nectar
Hover, wings pull petals into sky

II

In the center a bee's sting
On the ground dead ants
Where the fallout splinters.

We turn to glass
Crystal clink & chatter
Of the cocktail hour.

A code firmly in place,
A silo in the valley.

Drones pass the field
Gather sap from black branches.

Lady Macbeth to Wind

Turn wind, *turn,* she says–
A gesture
Rustle of the sparrow
A spider's web on the gatepost.

Free in the seconds before rain
Pellets shimmer into her eyes
Glass water–having crossed
The lake, washed on silk horizons.

Come fire, night–
Transformation in her veins
A ringed dove on the exuviae
Of a serpent.

The polar tides, the glacial drift
Slow the light's descent.
Light can sever flesh
& vapours can pierce skin–

Lost are some from the start.

Scotch, Is It?

Something I like to drink
Or something given to me at funerals
Or weddings, waiting for the bride & groom
To surface from the photo shoot?

The bitter taste of boarding school,
Friends who were kicked out for drinking too much
On a cool dorm Saturday night?
The chaser to go with pot and cigarettes?

The flame,
The orange heat on my tongue
A reminiscence of my grandfather,
Who toured the highlands in search

Of single malt, and my other grandfather,
Who never drank a drop. Teetotallers
Both in old age–hot water & honey.
Glass, the last rush of their lives.

The scent of amber,
As if on a hazy day I can walk
By the canal & smell fog
Or stare through clouds at night.

This bodied red heat, wood casks
Aged with bourbon.
On a cold night I return to the fire.

Love in the Time of Dioxin

"This urge, wrestle, resurrection of dry sticks,
Cut stems struggling to put down feet,
What saint strained so much,
Rose on such lopped limbs to a new life?"
Theodore Roethke

I Lines

so it is true
we knew each other
but forgot names
even in the best of company
this happens daily

torn fingernails, cuts in
wood, on thighs
coated with laughter
phantoms

we were at the center
a surface with scratches
& two points leading away

we could have been looking
from the zenith onto dotted valleys

we were flies gathered in clumps
on the broken window
peering out from shuttered casings

II Blow of Hammers

you with your visions
hammers

dark blows hitting skin

your bones withstand steel
your face contorts
you pour salt around the pentagram

to hear your arrhythmic heart beating
    (suicide pacts)

there is no comfort
    relief is a word
& the blows leave marks

malignancy in the bruises

III Wormwood

this plum in my hand is so ripe
it reminds me of yesterday
    there were bruises
    arguments
    cracks on the ceiling

we are now bent over
    with monoliths
    on our backs

the bough carries our marks
    carved into flesh & wood

reminders of the trail
without bread or salves

IV Descent

like silk burning, we fall
to the bottom

coiled, a lifeless mass
of wintry flesh & skin

with the banging overhead
we hear no answers, deposit
no hopes in the doorway

now we look through red eyes
into splintered sun
it is getting late

a cord around our feet
heads bowed down with weight

come morning, we collect
our charnel grief
& look through open windows

V Frost

all of it could be ours. the ripe
orchards for plucking, crates filled with fruit

& courtly favors from the sultan.
too bad, the lost time. past

this cold pane of glass we reach out
only to crack ice, split open veins.

this pulling back, this pulling
forward. testing the waters

for hidden rocks before diving.
daisies that wilt

in the wild. it could have been memorable
against the sea wall. spinning,

spinning, like a small whirlpool
to swallow scars. again

we linger, again we gather dust,
fashion a house from frost

VI Heart-Bone

the timbre of bark peeling
& pollen on the wings
of butterflies

there the earth creates its own sanctuary
our bodies collapse into wind
scattered like islands   floating
in salt water

the *I Ching* hexagrams show “Progress”
this time bears no ill-will
no iron traces or impurities
no carts that pull on blackened wings
salt licks our wounds
we will grow back
broken bone

it is only copper coin tossed–
a wish cast into fire

VII Vow

across the plains
thieves cut with razors
still we persevere
behind stone walls
we hear the echo

the open ground reveals
the crooked path
stones trail off
steps taken into dark

we vow to protect ourselves
to never let the hangman
gather rope

VIII Right Ventricle: Garden

but still I hear your name
from the wet pull of waves.
we look up at days, trace
the marks on our faces

cast a wish into fire
watch ash turn into life
the center of the garden.

we throw up our arms
walk down the trail
of resurrection roses.

we plant seeds & water them
lilies grow where the earth
turns over,

stones etched by wind & rain
what have we ever lost by dying?

Fidelity

(Translation of Paul Éluard's *Fidèle*)

Living in a calm town
Where the road turns long and hard
For a place of blood and tears.
We are pure.

The nights are hot and tranquil
And we guard for lovers
This precious heart
Between all: life-spirit.

Skill

(D) sign
si(G)n
(g) one
(d) na
dna

Fish

(Translation of Paul Éluard's *Poisson*)

Fish, swimmers, boats
Transform water.
Water is soft and moves only
For those who touch it.

The fish advances
Like a finger into a glove,
The swimmer dances slowly,
And the sail breathes.

But soft water moves
For those who touch it,
For the fish, the swimmer, the boat
That it carries
And carries along.

Driving

(Translation of Paul Éluard's *Conduire*)

The road is soon there.
At the road, the horse.

Prettier than the crow,
He requires a path.

Thin-legged, light hero
Who follows his master to rest.

The road is soon there:
We run, we trot, we walk
We stop ourselves.

No Amendment

And so clauses are constructed
For her, conditions for one
Or more children, unpublished books....

We draft a will around the dark table,
Stacks of books on shelves,
Leather chairs arranged to peer

Down at the city. Civility, code.
And deal done, black ink
Marks where my body will drop.

Bee's Edge

But it stings
& stings deep

cuts into flesh
radiates red pain

stung, I die
martyr to the hive

& genealogy

Herniated Disc

I

I know the word *supine,* the edge of scalpel,
The osteopath's blunt manipulations. I know
The angle of the sky, flat on the ground
Drugged, as waves of cloud pass by then winter.
I know the lung's breath horizontal
Column on column fallen, the lopsidedness
Of a wolf in some other skin. I know vanishing
Points, the way light splits into dark then back
If you stare at it too long. I know the spacious
Blue of day, the Gyproc's cracks.
The web stretching from corner to corner, dangling
Threads in the meditation room.
The smooth roll off bed, to ice & heat.

II

Supine is marrow, digs into the coccyx.
Supine waits & cannot stand.
Supine gimps along, stung by the eyes of angels.

Concinnity

Cells move with design, the cerebral, consonant
Flow of masters. Sheathes of grey dulse
A sea's salt answer, swerved magnetic fields
Axons & dendrites: a body's sentence.

Cells, the red-basalt churn of sound deep within a
Barrier. Cells with intelligence,
A road of vowel fragments pieced together in unheard replies.

The body will heal if....

Words break down, discs rearrange themselves
To forge a deeper mine. Half-missed syllables,
Misprisions of *time.*

Cell sounds that feed esophagus, gut, limb
Clash in the electron rush.

Spirit Intrusion II

Though words devour themselves
Like moths that glean no wisdom,

Though bone can crack and heal
Without losing its position,

Though the iron twang of consonance can trigger,
Beneath the marrow, a primordial turn,

The brain hears only what it wants to hear.

*

Bone-fragment: a word lost in the *mêlée.*
Bone-house: a word rediscovered.

Fragments fuse and slowly become whole.
The body absorbs bone, marrow, slivers
And realigns into new positions: shape-shifter.

Strength of armature, form, metre.
The clash and grind of "k" "d" "t"
Stuck in the protrusion.

Bone Lodge

This bug tic is a flicker of pain–
On my back, feet crossed to lighten
The harsh grind of nerve-pulse.

Wish: to hike over a mountain, or jump
With radiating jolts gone: discs, tibia,
Clavicle in alignment

Not one inch shorter or jutting from the column,
Nerve-vision from the breathing spine:
Message cortex unravelled

Along the mind's path.
Black-pressure, wings spread out,
Wings tucked in, as the nerve jounces.

Love in the Time of Dioxin II

the girl steps into the tattoo parlor
"truth" is on her body: trysts

now nameless
pain of ink

etched into skin: *forever*
she thinks, *I will not betray*

word from the past

a Japanese calligraph
between ribs & breasts

*

pain is a reflection
aftermath

–this is not it
& out the door

for a moment's pleasure
this is not it

body-scar
the ink prompt

*

live wire on flesh
"now" engraved
an eagle on his shoulder

Billy sports tattoos up & down
one a mirror of his girlfriend
another barbed wire
the night he was thrown in jail
he stayed dressed for fear

the indelible spots
insignia of skull & bones
cosa nostra, jail-house

her
a brief fling
from the library
her ex-boyfriend's name
seared, still as new, across
her coccyx

the buzzing fine-toothed needle
cuts with a drill's precision
injects ink near veins

the tattoo grows
fades
"now" blurs

a vowel squished
consonant smudged
the eagle will crease
at the wings

Snapshots

Linings ripped & minnows
Catch the suck & pull of lead
Ground without flowers

*

White Plains, NY
Blood-red leaves
In an evergreen field of glass

*

Tuscan hills
Caesar's breath floats
Lorenzo Medici's coat

Perfect Utility

In the afternoon rooks nest,
roosters rattle in the vineyard;
we walk past blood petals, turrets,

green groves & tiered earth;
wind that washes arms–
arteries hardened from diesel;

while deep in the hills
a man pulls a rusted scythe
from his Defender jeep,

ancient steel that brushes
against Chianti grapes,
flowers with Bacchus' seal.

San Gimignano, Italy

Catalan: Earth Marks

a door open to dark agate sea
a berth, beds stacked
privacy, or so it seemed
a journey to the birthplace
of Kabbalah, to Gaudi's Catalan
with mosaic spires & wax-drop castles

three boys stand on the train platform
watch land go by
summer over & blue sky in the air
tracks rattle wooden-framed windows
past dusty hills of Spain
heavy air of *Gitanes* &
Givenchy layered on posted letters

cool breeze, pellucid ocean
& non-stop travel
on salt-caked eyes
greasy hair, stale clothes
too tired to find nirvana
among narrow cobblestones
pale- & yellow-white of streets
across a park with shaded green
benches to catch one-eyed slumber

red wine & freedom
courses through the body

in the railroad station
worn wood chairs, white stucco designs

graffiti by the tracks:
Felix Gonzalez was here

Barcelona

Orpheus's Nightmare

This spring Cybele
Will come & Orpheus will know no name.

It could have been I
Who prayed for sunrise, or the talk of crickets.
Songbirds in the mute moonlight.

Too late the hours. The howl of timber wolves
Sharpens the nerve's impulse. I cannot sleep.

Day startles a child's play with its whisper
That drifts through winter ice against silver
that scatters into earth.

New Breed

"Dangerous smog levels today
wear ultraviolet protection"

hair catches fire by the roadside
carcasses of mad cows
burn with two-headed
frogs & hermaphroditic toads

the stone wet with cancer
with the blood of rocks, of insects
& us, taken into a centrifuge
spun fast, so as

to distill the virus
fish spawn in mercury
fatten in a month
on hormones

the man's face
now shining into quicksilver
flashes, fever rising....

Silhouette

Through dawn my eyes circle
to a cage by the river.
Still, the night pierces the living,
the wound left open, as the raven
races across the isthmus.

To locate a center, walk in circles.
The light of my body seeks
the quick mercury of our lives.
The tracks grow deep, paw prints in the dark,
don't turn back, don't turn your face
to the black sun.

Night Train

All aboard in the dead of winter. Crossing,
Crossing, the layers of ice that glisten
Like blood in the storm.

All board, the train runs past waterways
& mountain stillness.
All board, a hand reaches into night.

All aboard past the river's edge. We watch
From windows as wind catches.
Brings us, unbroken.

Come, cries the heron; the day is ended.
Come, cries the crow; the dark is now.

Earth Marks

hills pocked with firs
ancient enfilades of pine

basalt, slate
torc-curve of glacial

moraine-lines drawn
from the core

alluvial-flow, stonemason
the surface that erodes

crust of metal moves
crumbles loam

water cascade pushes
slowly into the forest bed

morass, butte, carved
and scored by a needle, slow, planet lines

Orpheus

no one *knows*
markers & stones
where the body lies

cut off
left
in a stream
rising
the slow
haze
as if it
could be *real*

our steps
reveal paths taken by strangers
traveling through the East
& West

now the wind
tunes bones
& far away
brings up the carcass
from the swamp

the earth
will sprout forget-me-nots

Black-Light Train

From the seaside tunnel, I
Walk into night. You stand waiting,
Your arms spread to the sky.

Passages cut hills where steel
Tracks follow the dark metal *clink* of sound.
Blue fire on axles leading us astray.

Now in the still air, a breath floats.
Light fades to dark, opens up again through fire,
The shell that washes on shore, still dry.

Reflection

Will it be black? I will not know
But I don't want to be dust,
Burned in a fire.

There is no amendment till
Hard rock crumbles into sea,
Leaving a shell washed
On a white shore
Below the sycamore
Covered with cold dew.

When the Door Opens

Could it be lysergic
& dopamine-induced
Visions, swirling circles,
God's design?

In the heat, white lines glow,
Grow wide or shrink
Or fuse into the distance.

Above the eye's track,
The strong-armed tricks
Of Gödel & Escher, who
Distort sequence & the frame.

For an instant we escape
Constraints: the boundary,
The childhood fall,
The clock's tick.

Slow nerves tingle.
We are black boxes
That receive and emit signals.
We hear our names.

Strange-Blessings

Again, light-filled shafts

Spirit-made blood returns

All to G-d, desire
    Dreamt

Walking, breath-turn
A radius, a slant of light

    So now it seems strange

The blessed heart, the open wound-heart:

Life, veins,   re-
                      New(al)

* * *

A General's Postscript

I go, steady in mind. I regain lost heights. I recall wandering
through the garden, veiled laughs by the orange blossoms
beside the hacienda, next to the cholla and the perpetual
stream. Little more. Days pass and I begin to fail. Nights are
longer and the early breaths of morning come quickly. I feel
you, as armies rush in. A light-blossom opens where I stumble.
I see a shaded silhouette, your face backlit, crimson lips.
These outdo the lusts of war. Here, where we are, measures
itself by the strokes of some hand: ashes to ashes, dust to dust.
My lips caress what is still us. As the light fades, I see you
walking in far fields, surrounded by white desert ghostflowers
in rows. Caesuras stun me with foreboding. Black blossoms
fill with a sound so dense it is heard by no one. *Come to me,*
I am yours. Come to me, I hear the bells ringing…. I will rest
in marble, beside the busts and armouries, with the cries of
youth, next to the General's visor. The ash of battle scatters.
I have seen the vast plains of armies scatter. I see what has
passed. You are there. The rest fades into nothing.

Ararat Lookout

I

I look onto Mt. Ararat's red stone,
feel the breeze from shanty towns,
crumbled walls & makeshift ceilings;
wind blows south the scent

of fresh oranges
& caterwauls of children
beside the tinted *Intourist* bus.

II

Poverty is the god,
Lenin an idol,
thin wine & black butter,
prisons & hammered minds.

Winter brings salt,
frost in the breast,
carries us into night.

On the hill a grove,
green nestled leaves
& the hotel for tourists–
the food so succulent here.

Cool air & mountain ridges.
The ark a memory
come through Persia,
the covenant that floated.

We hear the guns fire,
flints light the torch.
Roads gather, empty.

III

The twist of time.
Now red stone glitters
endless, an ocean.
The rock betrays.

A mother's fate,
to cut black ribbons,
make memories
fade into earth.

We walk on a tarred street
past Civil Guards, modern Cossacks
in an armored car–
radar signals & flags warning.

Across the desert
to the Georgian border,
with more fresh apples
or baked loaves.

Slate erodes where children
search for bread,
a board for a makeshift roof.
Silence startles Tartar ghosts.

Erevan, Armenia, 1991

Ob River

Bubble subterranean glass
& soothing cool sound

from the magma,
the shale lined with ash & salt.

A raptured wing,
a midnight hawk's flight.

Slowly eddying pools, light-
tinctured puddles, carve ice sculptures,

cut wave patterns.
Erosion slow

in the snow-chalice. Blood-beats
cascade from underground,

Mandelstam's chills & Solzhenitsyn's fever.
Exile in a gulag of frost.

The Spider

I

Lost in the grey air. Spindle of silk,
a distaff of floating web without anchor.
The spider leaves the earth, rises over a steeple,
drifting into light. A flying, silver, towering octopod–
God's sign. As I lie on my back, sundered,
unable to lift, the world revolves.
Invisible center up above, a point
recedes into nothingness. The weight of matter.

II

Still it spins. Macbeth's weïrd sisters see
the future, threads of what's to come.
The design only apparent now.
So my back is tics and nudges lodged in bone.
Crows and ravens circle in a *Luftwaffe*
formation above the lake.
To enter the cavity of ligament
and split chalk-bone that rips into blood.
The destiny of the clock. The spider spins,
weaves through night, some other intention.

Desire

It is a glance turned away,
that grows & grows insatiable–

a man stops by the sea shore, calm,
bends to look at splintered shells,

gathers skeletons of fish,
littered on an island of salt.

Death-bodies, dream-dodgers,
sailed to an icy land,

away from heat that splits.
Time will tell a clock from a vase,

hands that curve upwards,
lighting like flints

Reading Frost's *In The Clearing*

Tracks on a melting pond,
  The weight of boots.

In the heat, water glows.
  Ice thaws on a hot stove.

Water-worms move below thin sheets,
  Twist in accordance to law.

This is not day, this is not night.
  I sit & read Frost's inaugural poem to JFK.

A Nation-X truck passes. Is this assassination
  Part of the whole? The lines

Melt & move. Light squibs dart
  Into eyes, blinding. Last night

A fire, and today a blow-out fight–
  Words cast into glares. A curse, a nation.

Wrong time, wrong motion.

Where the Sun Beats

I/Aegean Heat

slow brush fire lights the mountain
the islanders stand watching
waves of black smoke smolder
it'll be here in a couple of days
they say, as they gather
by one-room houses cut into cliffs

the young have all left
winter brings rheumatism & arthritis
a crag-faced woman
sits in her white-washed home
with bottles of buttons on the table
we climb onto the lookout
a view of the conflagration

there is nothing to do
up the snake-path that drops
hundreds of feet to slate valleys
an hour down a steep grade, to town, to water
to buy a few noodles, fruit, or cheese

in the night drivers wind the road
drunk on retsina & ouzo

to survive one needs to be rugged
hard like the mountain
brush erupts, blazes

across Serifos, smoke
streams into lungs

ash-colored sky burns
as we leave on the *Flying Dolphin*
embered Paleohora, cacti
& sparse green desert-tufts

II/Near Augustus' Tomb

There is a certain quality of stone. Time-density. At corners, bridges, sculptures, roads, pediments. The Romans, well-dressed cosmopolitans, stand up for cappuccinos. Scooters rumble across the cityscape. Layers, pentimento, ash. As if we uncover with each stone some unknown. And the architectural facades. Classical, orderly, beyond Bacchus. Stones full of Rome. Where we turn, a mausoleum absorbs diesel fumes.

III/S. Pietro Epiphany

I walk in with
white orchids
for the dead

our bodies glide
swaying
to the pillar

by the eye of
the cupola, the melted bronze
of the Pantheon

which opens
walk down the nave
& apse, past the frescoes

& Pieta; works in the
mind of God begun–
"for a return

cast three sticks
into fire & light
the incense"

Reading the River from a Cessna

clackering of propellers
whish & whinge of geese
above scattered sections of ice

beneath a jigsaw puzzle
a white-cloud-stream

cracked earth-ribs vault open
huddled red-brown hills
ore spilt, veins ripped
crimson pockets of a tobacconist's dream

all wash on a horizon
chalk-cracked squares of earth
30,000 feet below iodine
residue of a hawk that cruises
ospreys & martens circle
the wild-eye grey-blue
aquiline coast

this, a broken wing
& salt on open ground
this, a swift with oil black feathers
that pulls from the center

Harvest

In an open field
crates of apples.

Leaves furled & stalks crunched
into lettuce-heaps.

Roots draw up to ground
junk-metals thrown

into the river, near the mountain
with steel mills on its base.

Dawnwind
blows past crops

& furrows fill with farmers.
They move in as bonefrost

whitens the skin of earth-fruit,
hardened & ready

Ocean

Swish through weeds
Past the floating silver beads

Swish by the sand
Into the cold, human hand

White-belly on the shore
An aluminum reel

Cruiser boats with ultrasound
Map the undertow.

Bring the Rain on

Smooth glass, black tides glisten,
past weeds beavers
dive to a water lodge.
Trees buckle on the log strap
–open hearts, pine & conifer,
piled onto an unseemly kiva.

I scoop up earth: an ancient bird rib
caged in the clay-casket,
& wings' slow decay. Loons call,
as if to urge, *no, move on.* I wait for you
on the low trail beside the ten-foot
sunflower stretching from lake shore
up to the Weeping Walking Willow
& Korean blossom.

The horticultist lives here,
careful to bring up roots.
Ore from earth-memory.
The season starts early,
patterns of grape vines,
black-eyed susans & azaleas.
Lush, thick, wax-green stalks extend from
wind into basal ground

Borders

Over bog-holes
In the deadfall patch,
Pine, maple & spruce.

We take another walk
In woods
Where other worlds begin.

We cross the wide
Space–no return–
Mountains, streams.

Sun reaches fronds,
The cackle, *crawk*
Of unseen ravens,

Red-breasted robins & shrike.
Echoes surround.
Multiple chirps

From all angles,
From the split branches
Above. The rush

Of no-thought, no-dream,
As we walk farther
Onto the hogs-back,

Past the turbid
Stream, an oxbow
That widens

On the Coast

Night fills with supernal light
Sparse trees, cliffs & children in small boats.
Silence spreads. You look at me through
A blue glass lens, lean into my embrace.

We are light giving onto hard ground.
The rock garden an escarpment, terra cotta pots.
The trail leads to the ocean's edge, our faces
Reflected into an Escher infinity, a Möbius
Of curves.

The ablutions of our time: a lyric or a bow
Of light. We look to obsidian tides,
Suddenly hear the whaler's harp.

We will wade in deeper....

Across stark basalia. In the distance,
A beam flashes, isolation of junipers
& bald rock.

Gatineau Hills

We drive past farmhouses,
knotted hills with green spires.
I know we've passed

the open window.
You say, *come quick,* & I race, knowing
day fades fast, black clouds engulf.

The roads curves held onto, the car stalls,
river air rises, & we wait:
hungry, bones chilled.

Past the *Outaouais* bridge,
we carry ourselves in
black tides, the mismanagement

of lives: finished friendships,
cuts left open–
green hills removed.

No, it *couldn't* wait, & I look back:
parking tickets, tenements,
rat race first. *Take the long way,* you say.

Boreal

We look out onto lakes,
thrushes, bulrushes & small perch
that glide on mirrored light.

Like waterfalls, runnels from streams,
or glaciers carved in tidal pools,
we let out gathered steam.

The urge to dive down & bring up
sediment, lily roots, green algae,
spawn of two-headed frogs–half in,

half-out & moving into nether.
So this water is clear,
the air full of leaves, waves rock

driftwood onto shore.
Two red-breasted blackbirds fly together
toward Algonquin.

This flight over old stone,
coal that splinters, brings us
into night: still, lost in the center.

East End

the *Dunkin' Donuts* is a smoke-cloud by the metro
the *Boules de Neige* stocks our Japanese incense
& the blues bar serves dirty beer at night

across St. Denis street up to the East End,
near our rickety apartment,
snow drifts through the wood door

I feel the artery running through this city.
outside, a man is dragged, drugged
he's set in flashing red *Urgence* lights
near the *Fameux* Smoked Meat restaurant
the silver *Galaxie* diner

I drink without you

The Panther–Central Park Zoo

(After Rilke)

He gazes into the park from behind
steel bars and concrete walls. Passing cars
a constant hum. He breathes
black tar and sees children with stones.

Metal bears strike clock-bells as he skulks
in his cage. His supple stride turns
a very small circle, pivots like a steel-toed dancer
about a center, where strength is undone.

When the crowd dwindles his eyes open
onto Africa, across yellow plains
and savannah... his limbs poise
for a moment then slink into the city.

Diary of a Journalist

Today in Calcutta somebody died.
Today in Madrid a bomb was discovered.
Today in Tokyo gas leaks in the suburbs.
Today in Colorado blood was discovered in Tylenol.
Today a white locust washed the crops of Jordan
  with genetically engineered dust.
Today a spaniel was born with three heads, to better
  play the part.
Today an attendant bought bread at K-Store then
  murdered his secretary.
Today a woman appealed the abuse of parents, code,
  and body marks to no avail.
Today my back cracked, a tiny microcosm of strife.
Today Jupiter's roving spot was seen in the North.
Today my hurt centered one inch to the left.
Today Nostradamus's 18th prophecy took place.
Today Nostradamus's 20th prophecy took seed.
Today the future began 200 years ago in Rome.
Today Black Fever still exists.
Today two is not unquestionably two.
Today Cambridge is a nuclear reactor.
Today a woman broke her jaw on the Great Wall.
Today the Spanish woman I kissed is married with
  children not mine.
Today the catacombs are still open.

Phanerothyme

A man knows the secret is unspoken: a spontaneous transmission, imperceptible, immaculate, like a pearl. Mystery of the four senses: being, void, the absolute, the invisible. With the corners of the globe charted, there are only the isles of an interior journey.

Words could self-animate, take over the mind. Deranged at the outset, he divulged no cause or reason. If there really is a meaning, it must reside in the scriptural appearance of "Alef," the holy stone. Gilgamesh and Uruk still exist. A palimpsest of the original, bright color fades into technological innovation.

If he shook your hand, would you know if it's him, or his double? The meeting of minds melts the fractal space, reverberates through iron. After blitzing wildly like an elk, he dreamt of her face in the light, the cave, and the shadows. He stirred the wind with stars, against the backdrop of a cloudy sea.

Time, most weary of itself, is without name. The hourglass quickly fills with wonder. Where does all this lead? *X moves towards its infinite series....*

He tries to find the missing link.
If there is a way, it would seem to be through theories of the Absurd.
A graph reveals the indigence of signs & symbols.

Tail of the Tiger

Zen echoes, song of Gampopa above the sloping hills

Heads bowed & rice wine
The slow ceremony

I become a part of it

With a pin in my stomach
I carve my initials into earth

*

I slice into shadows, dark nights

Expiration & regeneration. A leaf falls from the poplar
A breath. Stick-bone corpses, radium instead of carbon

Karme Choling, wind chimes
A butterfly's wings ripple
Alter polar winds

Echo the pulse of running water
Tokyo & Tibet
Tangerine on tongue

New Dawn II

I

Dawn rose white, blue, yellow
    unheard, untouched
    light-ripples on pine needles
    jackrabbits across snow

from the island lookout: hidden tricksters
    crows

    Renaissance music plays & the gyre turns
    west to east, up to down
    above each of us here

    in Israel
    in Russia
    in Pakistan

the sun shrinks to human measure
our failed grasp

II

child: *why is the stone carved with silence*
the sea hot blue, orange, violet, indigo?

this prison, this spectrum
a multitude, time-ripples

    I wait for your light, it is the body on this page

    how do we read this covered ground
    specter of dust & bright powder?

I watch your feet grind
grey-crusted tracks in the snow

Measure

With the white-out I saw nothing.
Not the blue sky, not the earth.

Each merged into blur. The layers
Of frost we sprout from. The sheen

Of ice we carry in our bones
Gives way into night. Dark

Creeps through vessels & roots. The source
Of our light is scattered: slow sea

Cascades onto rocks, a missing
Puzzle-piece on the linoleum floor.

We too find our measure in small things: a box

Of chocolates, a letter from Florence,
A broad smile. Too long between meals,

The kind that really fill the body,
Kindle the blood's fire.

Light pours through windows,
Peels across shutters. It crosses

The floor and bisects our living. To one side
We blossom cherry buds, to the other

We draw in a single gasp

Drawing Near the Sun

Waiting on shore, I find
foam washed onto sand,
a wave on the rock face.
And now, you leap,
quick to cut down
the sails on the horizon.

We still seek each other.
The white-wash & bric-a-brac
of our journey: ablated stones,
driftwood, & quartz.

*

Always, you say, & draw near the sun,
the steady progress
of our hands across each other.

You search for the center.
Continue till you are my body & I
your source

Acknowledgements

Acknowledgements are due to the editors of the following, where these poems originally appeared:

Abiko Quarterly (Japan), The Antigonish Review, Asheville Poetry Review, Burning Bush (Ireland), Cake Train, California Quarterly, Carquinez Poetry Review, Chaffin Journal, CV2, Descant, Diner, Dirty Goat, Distillery, Eclipse, Event, The Fiddlehead, Fire (UK), Illuminations, International Poetry Review, Limestone, Maisonneuve, Matrix, Nashwaak Review, /nor, Nth Position, Poetry Greece, Poetry NZ (New Zealand), The Potomac Review, Prairie Fire, Prism International, Semicolon (UK), Shearsman (UK), Soliloquies, Spoon River Review, Sulphur River Review, Runes, The Sow's Ear, Queen's Quarterly, and *Vallum.*

"Measure" and "Where the Sun Beats" won respectively the First and Third Place Orion Prizes for Poetry.

"Love in the Time of Dioxin II" won the Ray Burrell Award for Poetry.

"Catalan" received the Warren Keith Wright Prize.

"Harvest" won the Milton Acorn Prize.

Sections of "Love in the Time of Dioxin" won the Irving Layton Award for Poetry.

"The Spider" and "New Dawn II" received commendation for the International Hanna Davoren Competition.

"Boreal" was printed as a broadside for the Acorn-Livesay Festival. "Harvest" appeared as part of an audio CD from Paper Tiger Media (Australia), and "Diary of a Journalist" was released as a CD track by *Gargoyle. Informal Measures,* a chapbook by above/ground press, featured several of these poems. Some of these poems also appeared in the following anthologies: *Short Fuse: Global Anthology of New Fusion Poetry, A Last Showy Jive Anthology,* and *Cherish our Heritage Anthology.*

Joshua Auerbach was born in Toronto and has lived in Canada, the US, and Europe. A graduate of McGill University, he has also attended Harvard University and Université de Grenoble. His work has been published internationally and has won several awards, including *This Magazine's* Great Canadian Literary Hunt and the Orion Prize. He is co-founding editor of *Vallum magazine,* and directs VSFAALE, a registered charity that promotes aesthetic awareness through live events and print publications.

100%

This book has been printed on 100% post consumer waste paper, certified Eco-logo and processed chlorine free.